WRITE THE VISION: HABAKKUK 2:2

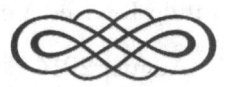

Pastor Dr. William Standifer, Sr.

WRITE THE VISION: HABAKKUK 2:2

Copyright © 2009 by Pastor Dr. William Standifer, Sr.
and Dr. Juanita Standifer- Woodson

All rights reserved. No part of this publication may be reproduced, stored in a retrieval system or transmitted in any way by any means, electronic, mechanical, photocopy, recording or otherwise without the prior permission of the author except as provided by USA copyright law.

All Scripture quotations are taken from the
Holy Bible King James Version (KJV). All rights reserved.

2nd Printing Revised Version

August 2016

3rd Printing 2022

ISBN 978-1-7330800-8-8

Acknowledgements

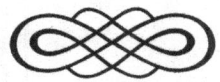

In Loving Memory of the late

Pastor/Dr. William Standifer Sr. (1938-2021)

First, we thank Almighty God for the inspiration to write this book.

We also thank God for the Bible teaching that we received under the late Bishop W. T. Phillips and Overseer James H. Durham.

A very special thanks to my daughter, Dr. Juanita Standifer,-Woodson Evangelist Tangie Anderson and Mrs. Brenda Nichols, who worked tirelessly with me to put my writings in printed form.

And most important, thanks to each of you who will hear and receive this Word of God.

Table of Contents

The Coming Nuclear Holocaust! 1

My Personal Testimony 3

The Attack and Invasion 7

Israel 11

The Fall of America and Judgment 20

Hope of the Righteous 24

Great Tribulation 26

Terrorism 28

Black Gold 36

China Emerges as a Great Nation 41

About the Author 45

THE COMING NUCLEAR HOLOCAUST!

Throughout world history we find wars being fought. Usually they were waged over land disputes, territorial ambitions and sometimes spontaneous incidents. Some of these incidents were purposely staged in order to have a justifiable excuse to begin hostilities. From ancient time to the present wars have come about over many and varied circumstances.

A few that come to mind; the attack on the USS Maine in Cuba (considered by many to be contrived) was used as a justifiable reason for the Spanish American War. Of course, we know World War II came about in large part due to territorial ambitions and conquest by Germany and Japan. The Korean War began with communist North Korea invading democratic South Korea. The Vietnam conflict dated back to pre-world War II and was waged by what later was proven to be the masses who wanted freedom from foreign control.

We know that the September 11, 2001 (commonly referred to as 9/11) attacks brought about the war on terrorists in Afghanistan. And of course the Iraqi War was based on the belief that Sadaam Hussein was hoarding weapons of mass destruction.

We have outlined just a few wars going back roughly one hundred years. There were so many others involving many nations around the world.

This book was written to shed some light on the end time war or wars, and the effect on our nation and the world. God has revealed in His word the events leading up to and culminating in the return of our Lord and Savior Jesus Christ to the earth. This we hope to have shown through scripture. If God says something - it will be done and done the way and in the time that He says it will be done!

MY PERSONAL TESTIMONY

To begin, I would like to give a personal testimony. During the year of 1963 I became sick and tired of the lifestyle I was living. Drugs, alcohol, fornication, and partying were the order of the day. One night while feeling in the depths of despair I went on my knees in the bedroom, of which my live in girlfriend and I shared. I think she was at work on this particular night. So, being alone I poured my heart out to God and asked him if there was a better way of life than what I was living.

He answered me later, if not that night, soon after, in a vision on my bedroom ceiling. First, there appeared the hand of an angel as if to direct my attention to something. Then the scene changed as if a projector was being used. The next scene was the Bible opened up and all a glitter. There were two other scenes that were taken from my memory but I've always felt that God would bring them back in time. However, inspired by this vision I began to read the Bible, notably the New Testament.

While reading the Bible, I would at times take a good stiff drink of whiskey thinking this would calm my mind and I could get a better understanding of what I was reading. On one occasion while doing this I fell into a semi-conscience state and heard a loud voice saying,

"Repent, repent of your sins!" Of course it was a harrowing experience and I knew that the drinking had to go. I made a New Year's Eve vow to quit and God enabled me to honor it. One day on the job I made a vow to quit smoking, (one and a half packs a day) and God blessed me to quit by simply taking away the taste.

On this job, I met a saved deacon by the name of Edward Jackson. I was drawn to him because of his lifestyle. I never heard any profanity come out of his mouth, no lighting up or ugly joke telling. As we got better acquainted, I began to share with him my experiences. He began to tell me about Holiness and invited me to church.

One Sunday afternoon I was home alone. Everyone else had gone to the movies or somewhere. I went downstairs and got into this 1953 Chrysler that my uncle had given me and just started driving east on 59th Street (Chicago). I looked to my left and saw this little store front church. Then it dawned on me that this was the church that Edward Jackson had invited me to come.

I parked, went in and discovered they were getting ready to dismiss after an afternoon service. At the behest of my friend, I went up for prayer and was asked to come to Bible class on Wednesday to which I readily agreed. On returning to that session I sat on the last pew in the back of the church.

The Pastor was teaching from the book of Isaiah 53:1-5 (KJV): Who hath believed our report? and to whom is the arm of the LORD revealed? For he shall grow up before him as a tender plant, and as a root out of a dry ground: he hath no form nor comeliness; and when we shall see him, *there is* no beauty that we should desire him. He is despised and rejected of men; a man of sorrows, and acquainted with grief: and we hid as it were our faces from him; he was despised, and we esteemed him not. Surely he hath borne our griefs, and carried our sorrows: yet we did esteem him stricken, smitten of God, and afflicted. But he *was* wounded for our transgressions, *he was* bruised for our iniquities: the chastisement of our peace *was* upon him; and with his stripes we are healed.

As the altar call was made I felt like a huge weight was sitting on me. (The devil didn't want to let go.) Finally, with all of the strength I could muster, I stood upon my feet. Upon standing, my legs just began to take me to the altar. I was asked by the Pastor, "Do you believe the report?" I opened my mouth and the words just came out. "Yes, I believe that this is the only way that a man can be

saved." To this he asked, "When would you like to be baptized?" My reply was "as soon as possible." It was that night on March 31, 1964 in the back of a drafty, old store front church, in the city of Chicago, Illinois that I repented of my sins and was baptized in the name of the Lord Jesus Christ.

Not many days after my baptism, God filled me with the Holy Ghost and I brought my family and my live-in girlfriend with me to church. We were joined in holy matrimony in May 1964. She received salvation the same year and the family was united to the church. To the five existing children were added two more, these all being raised in the church. The eldest son, now a Bishop in Chicago, Illinois; my wife and the eldest daughter (both deceased) served in the ministry; my youngest daughter, a Prophetess and having received her Doctorate Degree, is working with underprivileged families in the state of Illinois.

We find in 1st John 1:5-10 (KJV) these words: This then is the message which we have heard of him, and declare unto you, that God is light, and in him is no darkness at all. If we say that we have fellowship with him, and walk in darkness, we lie, and do not the truth: But if we walk in the light, as he is in the light, we have fellowship one with another, and the blood of Jesus Christ his Son cleanseth us from all sin. If we say that we have no sin, we deceive ourselves, and the truth is not in us. If we confess our sins, he is faithful and just to forgive us *our* sins, and to cleanse us from all unrighteousness. If we say that we have not sinned, we make him a liar, and his word is not in us.

As we walk in the light of God's word we are continuously being washed in the blood. Concerning the church, Paul wrote in Ephesians 4:11-13 (KJV): And he gave some apostles, and some prophets, and some evangelists; and some pastors and teachers; For the perfecting of the Saints, for the work of the ministry, for the edifying of the Body of Christ; Till we all come in the unity of the faith, and of the knowledge of the Son of God, unto a perfect man, unto the measure of the stature of the fullness of Christ.

As we yield ourselves totally to God He will perfect us in Him. Paul said also in Ephesians 5:27 (KJV), "That Christ is to present the church to himself not having spot of wrinkle or any such thing; but that it should be Holy and without blemish."

Our prayer to God is that this book will be a blessing and will cause the readers (especially those who do not know the Lord) to stop and consider and to hold fast as we see that Great Day approaching. God said "Write the Vision" and we have endeavored to do so in all meekness and humility.

The Attack and Invasion

In the year of 1965 or 1966, God showed me a vision.

In the vision my wife was standing with me. A voice would speak out a series of numbers. These I understood to be coordinates on the globe. Each time this would happen my wife would ask, "Where is that?" I would answer, "That's such and such a place." Then there would be a loud explosion. This continued for a time of the numbers being spoken, her asking where it was, my answers and the explosions. Finally, after a round of this and her asking, "Where is that?" I answered, "That's right overhead! Get down!" We fell to the ground but there was no explosion. Instead, the scene changed.

The name of a Soviet city in the Ukraine, "Kiev" began to appear. It began small but grew larger and larger in three dimensional letters. This made me know that this city would be instrumental in events leading up to an attack on America. Not only will we be attacked but we will be invaded also and some will be carried away captive to other countries.

Somewhere around this time I also had a dream of being on a ship with a bunch of captives heading for Russia. Many years later a Pastor friend shared a similar dream with me only he felt they were being taken to Africa.

I feel that God is giving the nation over into the hands of its enemies. When Israel obeyed God, He gave them victory over their enemies. When they disobeyed and turned to idolatry He gave them into the hands of their enemies. I've heard a number of believers tell of having dreams or visions of foreign troops coming ashore on our coasts. Some believe they will also simply come across the southern border.

Even now the Department of National Security is concerned about various types of weaponry, chemical agents; even dirty A-bombs, being smuggled in through shipping containers or other means. When our nation is so dependent on imports, (this because so much of our industry is being moved to foreign countries) then we open ourselves up to such things as children's toys colored with lead paint, which was banned many years ago in this country. We know the standards in other nations are far below ours when it comes to public safety.

We import fruits and vegetables from countries that use pesticides that are banned in the USA. We depend on other countries to manufacture everything from steel, clothing, shoes, televisions, appliances and probably electronic components used in our Nation's defense systems. All of this as a result of big businesses closing American plants and going overseas for dirt cheap labor (some believe to be the work of prisoners).

It's obvious that the "fat cats" don't care about the American working class. The textile industry along with most of the steel industry, furniture manufacturing, shoemaking and other crafts, export the jobs and use cost as the reason. Nevertheless, they import these products back here and expect the American consumers to buy them. It would be a great day if the American people would refuse and tell them to sell them where they make them. If people don't have jobs and income, how can they buy products?

Let us remember that many of these so called global companies were built on the backs of American labor. In the early years of industrialization in this country workers toiled under appalling conditions. Child labor laws had to be passed to protect even the children. The stock yards (slaughter houses), steel mills, coal mines, textile mills and so many other industries, (lets not forget the auto industry) had to be forced through labor union pressure and government laws to make meaningful changes. As large corporations grew and profits sky rocketed the main emphasis was on the bottom line. This, my friend, is called greed.

The Apostle Paul said in 1st Timothy 6:10; "For the love of money is the root of all evil." It wasn't enough to be a good profitable and stable business, greed dictated the need to cut jobs and move factories to third and fourth world nations.

One of the top AFL-CIO officers said on a radio talk show (somewhere around 1971-1972) that the aim of the big corporations was to get the American workers on the same level with the rest of the world's workers. In other words, the things the American workers enjoyed such as, home ownership, cars, health benefits, and good education for our children would for the most part dissolve away. This would leave the haves (rich) and the have-nots (poor working class) eliminating the middle class.

Just look at the situation today!

In 1992 the USA threatened to raise the tariffs on French imported wines. France immediately said they would retaliate against American imports. Upon hearing this in the news, God brought to my mind the scripture in Rev.6:5-6 (KJV): And when he had opened the third seal, I heard the third beast say, Come and see. And I beheld, and lo a black horse; and he that sat on him had a pair of balances in his hand. And I heard a voice in the midst of the four beasts say, A measure of wheat for a penny, and three measures of barley for a penny; and *see* thou hurt not the oil and the wine.

This was soon after the desert storm war in Kuwait and Iraq over oil. The USA uses the conflict in Iraq as fighting against terrorism and the freedom of the people there. But remove oil from the equation and let's ask ourselves, "would we be there?"

When we look at the rapid growth and progression of China and India and their insatiable thirst for oil, we know that the war pots are boiling. Both of these nations along with Pakistan have nuclear weapons. Iran and North Korea are on the verge of obtaining the same.

ISRAEL

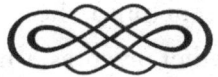

The 38th chapter of Ezekiel spells out nations that would come against Israel in the latter years.

Gog and Magog (considered as Russia by historians); Persia, which we know today is Iran, their leader having declared that Israel should be wiped off the map, this while declaring that they are pushing toward the development of nuclear weapons. Ethiopia and Libya are also named as allies along with Gomer and Togarmah (believed to be Turkey) and some other Eurasian peoples.

All these nations are coming together against tiny Israel. When you look at the odds then you know that only God can save Israel. At present only the USA and Britain are pledging to stand with Israel. God said He would bring all nations against Israel.

Israel was reestablished as a nation in 1948. This happened after being scattered into all nations in 70 A.D. by the Romans, and also after Israel rejected her Messiah and Savior. But God had already promised hundreds of years before this took place that He would restore them into their own land.

We read in Jeremiah 16:14-15 (KJV): Therefore, behold, the days come, saith the LORD, that it shall no more be said, The LORD liveth, that brought up the children of Israel out of the land of Egypt; But, The LORD liveth, that brought up the children of Israel from the land of the north, and from all the lands whither he had driven them: and I will bring them again into their land that I gave unto their fathers.

Right here we want to note the words of Jesus. Matthews 23:37-39 (KJV): O Jerusalem, Jerusalem, *thou* that killest the prophets, and stonest them which are sent unto thee, how often would I have gathered thy children together, even as a hen gathereth her chickens under *her* wings, and ye would not! Behold, your house is left unto you desolate. For I say unto you, Ye shall not see me henceforth, till ye shall say, Blessed *is* he that cometh in the name of the Lord.

This was prior to them being driven out of the land. They have been restored but are not yet a God fearing nation. That will change when only a remnant is left.

Isaiah 1:9 (KJV) reads: Except the LORD of hosts had left unto us a very small remnant, we should have been as Sodom, *and* we should have been like unto Gomorrah.

Paul wrote in Romans 9:27-28 (KJV): Esaias also crieth concerning Israel, Though the number of the children of Israel be as the sand of the sea, a remnant shall be saved: For he will finish the work, and cut *it* short in righteousness: because a short work will the Lord make upon the earth.

We find in Romans 11:1-5 (KJV): I say then, Hath God cast away his people? God forbid. For, I also am an Israelite, of the seed of Abraham, *of* the tribe of Benjamin. God hath not cast away his people which he foreknew. Wot ye not what the scripture saith of Elias? How he maketh intercession to God against Israel, saying, Lord, they have killed thy prophets, and digged down thine altars; and I am left alone, and they seek my life. But what saith the answer of God unto him? I have reserved to myself seven thousand men, who have not bowed the knee to the image *of* Baal. Even so then at this present time also there is a remnant according to the election of grace.

Romans 11:11 (KJV): I say then, Have they stumbled that they should fall? God forbid: but *rather* through their fall salvation *is* come unto the Gentiles, for to provoke them to jealousy.

He said further in Romans 11:17-27 (KJV): And if some of the branches be broken off, and thou, being a wild olive tree, wert graffed in among them, and with them partakest of the root and fatness of the olive tree; Boast not against the branches. But if thou boast, thou bearest not the root, but the root thee. Thou wilt say then, The branches were broken off, that I might be graffed in. Well; because of unbelief they were broken off, and thou standest by faith. Be not highminded, but fear: For if God spared not the natural branches, take heed lest he also spare not thee. Behold therefore the goodness and severity of God: on them which fell, severity; but toward thee, goodness, if thou continue in *his* goodness: otherwise thou also shalt be cut off. And they also, if they abide not still in unbelief, shall be graffed in: for God is able to graff them in again. For if thou wert cut out of the olive tree which is wild by nature, and wert graffed contrary to nature into a good olive tree: how much more shall these, which be the natural branches, be graffed into their own olive tree? For I would not, brethren, that ye should be ignorant of this mystery, lest ye should be wise in your own conceits; that blindness in part is happened to Israel, until the fullness of the Gentiles be come in. And so all Israel shall be saved: as it is written, There shall come out of Zion the Deliverer, and shall turn away ungodliness from Jacob: For this *is* my covenant unto them, when I shall take away their sins.

Let's look at the writing of Moses concerning God giving the land to Israel in the first place. Deuteronomy 9:3-6 (KJV) reads; Understand therefore this day, that the LORD thy God *is* he which goeth over before thee; *as* a consuming fire he shall destroy them, and he shall bring them down before thy face: so shalt thou drive them out, and destroy them quickly, as the LORD hath said unto thee. Speak not thou in thine heart, after that the LORD thy God hath cast them out from before thee, saying, For my righteousness the LORD hath brought me in to possess this land: but for the wickedness of these nations the LORD doth drive them out from before thee. Not for thy righteousness, or for the uprightness of thine heart, dost thou go to possess their land: but for the wickedness of these nations the LORD thy God doth drive them out from before thee, and that he may perform the word which the LORD sware unto thy fathers, Abraham, Isaac, and Jacob. Understand therefore, that the LORD thy God giveth thee not this good land to possess it for thy righteousness; for thou art a stiff necked people.

In verse 6, Moses is reminding Israel that it wasn't because of their goodness that they inherited the land but His promise (God's) to their forefathers.

Centuries later, we find them being taken into captivity. Israel was taken into Assyria, and Judah into Babylon. This happened in spite of continual warnings from the prophets, to turn from idolatry and wickedness or suffer the consequences.

Yet we find in Nehemiah's prayer in Nehemiah 1:8-9 (KJV): Remember, I beseech thee, the word that thou commandedst thy servant Moses, saying, If ye transgress, I will scatter you abroad among the nations: But *if* ye turn unto me, and keep my commandments, and do them; though there were of you cast out unto the uttermost part of the heaven, yet will I gather them from thence, and will bring them unto the place that I have chosen to set my name there.

So, we find even in their backslidings and disobedience, God would hear them when they repented and cried out to Him. While we're talking about God's dealing with Israel, let us not forget Paul's message of them being blinded in part for the Gentiles sake and that we are not to boast against the branches. Through faith we are able to be grafted into the natural tree, this because of the Gospel.

In Mark 16:15-16 (KJV) we find what is known as the great commission. The words of the Lord Jesus: And he said unto them, Go ye into all the world, and preach the gospel to every creature. He that believeth and is baptized shall be saved; but he that believeth not shall be damned.

We find in Peter's message on the day of Pentecost these words; Acts 2:38-39 (KJV): Then Peter said unto them, Repent, and be baptized every one of you in the name of Jesus Christ for the remission of sins, and ye shall receive the gift of the Holy Ghost. For the promise is unto you, and to your children, and to all that are afar off, *even* as many as the Lord our God shall call.

This is the fulfilling of God's promise to Abraham in Genesis 12:2-3 (KJV): And I will make of thee a great nation, and I will bless thee, and make thy name great; and thou shalt be a blessing: And I will bless them that bless thee, and curse him that curseth thee: and in thee shall all families of the earth be blessed.

This promise to Abraham is directly connected to the salvation of all mankind through the Gospel. Non-Jewish Christians are Abraham's seed by faith. We are grafted into the natural tree through faith in God's word. Hallelujah!

This promise could only come through the Messiah. Isaiah 11:10 (KJV) states: And in that day there shall be a root of Jesse, which shall stand for an ensign of the people; to it shall the Gentiles seek: and his rest shall be glorious.

Isaiah 7:14 (KJV) states: Therefore the Lord himself shall give you a sign; Behold, a virgin shall conceive, and bear a son, and shall call his name Immanuel.

We find this repeated by the angel to Joseph in Matthew 1:21-23 (KJV): And she shall bring forth a son, and thou shalt call his name JESUS: for he shall save his people from their sins. Now all this was done, that it might be fulfilled which was spoken of the Lord by the prophet, saying, Behold, a virgin shall be with child, and shall bring forth a son, and they shall call his name Emmanuel, which being interpreted is, God with us.

Isaiah known as the eagle eye prophet said further in Isaiah 9:6-7 (KJV): For unto us a child is born, unto us a son is given: and the government shall be upon his shoulder: and his name shall be called Wonderful, Counselor, The mighty God, The everlasting Father, The Prince of Peace. Of the increase of *his* government and peace *there shall be* no end, upon the throne of David, and upon his kingdom, to order it, and to establish it with judgment and with justice from henceforth even for ever. The zeal of the LORD of hosts will perform this.

The prophet Micah even told us where He would be born. Micah 5:2 (KJV): But thou, Bethlehem Ephratah, though thou be little among the thousands of Judah, *yet* out of thee shall he come forth unto me *that is* to be ruler in Israel; whose goings forth *have been* from of old, from everlasting.

Isaiah 40:3 (KJV) tells us of the coming of John the Baptist: The voice of him that crieth in the wilderness, Prepare ye the way of the LORD, make straight in the desert a highway for our God.

In Isaiah 40:9-11 (KJV) we read: O Zion, that bringest good tidings, get thee up into the high mountain; O Jerusalem, that bringest good tidings, lift up thy voice with strength; lift *it* up, be not afraid; say unto the cities of Judah, Behold your God! Behold, the Lord GOD will come with strong hand, and his arm shall rule for him: behold, his reward *is* with him, and his work before him. He shall feed his flock like a shepherd: he shall gather the lambs with his arm, and carry them in his bosom, and shall gently lead those that are with young.

These prophecies were made some seven hundred years before the coming of the Messiah Israel rejected Him because He did not restore the Kingdom of Israel from under Roman rule. This was not to be a part of His "first coming".

In Hebrews 2:9 (KJV) we read: But we see Jesus, who was made a little lower than the angels for the suffering of death, crowned with glory and honour; that he by the grace of God should taste death for every man.

In Hebrews 2:14-18 (KJV) we read: Forasmuch then as the children are partakers of flesh and blood, he also himself likewise took part of the same; that through death he might destroy him that had the power of death, that is, the devil; And deliver them who through fear of death were all their lifetime subject to bondage. For verily he took not on *him the nature of* angels; but he took on *him* the seed of Abraham. Wherefore in all things it behoved him to be made like unto *his* brethren, that he might be a merciful and faithful high priest in things *pertaining* to God, to make reconciliation for the sins of the people. For in that he himself hath suffered being tempted, he is able to succor them that are tempted.

Paul wrote in II Corinthians 5:19 (KJV): To wit, that God was in Christ, reconciling the world unto himself, not imputing their trespasses unto them; and hath committed unto us the word of reconciliation.

Paul further stated in Hebrews 4:14-16 (KJV): Seeing then that we have a great high priest, that is passed into the heavens, Jesus the Son of God, let us hold fast *our* profession. For we have not an high priest which cannot be touched with the feeling of our infirmities; but was in all points tempted like as *we are, yet* without sin. Let us therefore come boldly unto the throne of grace that we may obtain mercy, and find grace to help in time of need.

Let's look at Hebrews 5:1-10 (KJV): For every high priest taken from among men is ordained for men in things *pertaining* to God, that he may offer both gifts and sacrifices for sins: Who can have compassion on the ignorant, and on them that are out of the way; for that he himself also is compassed with infirmity. And by reason hereof he ought, as for the people, so also for himself, to offer for sins. And no man taketh this honour unto himself, but he that is called of God, as *was* Aaron. So also Christ glorified not himself to be made an high priest; but he that said unto him, Thou art my Son, to day have I begotten thee. As he saith also in another place, Thou *art* a priest for ever after the order of Melchisedec. Who in the days of his flesh, when he had offered up prayers and supplications with strong crying and tears unto him that was able to save him from death, and was heard in that he feared; Though he were a Son, yet learned he obedience by the things which he suffered; And being made perfect, he became the

author of eternal salvation unto all them that obey him; Called of God an high priest after the order of Melchisedec.

Through him God ushered in a new dispensation. We find in

Hebrews 7:19-28 (KJV): For the law made nothing perfect, but the bringing in of a better hope *did*; by the which we draw nigh unto God. And inasmuch as not without an oath he was made priest: (For those priests were made without an oath; but this with an oath by him that said unto him, The Lord sware and will not repent, Thou art a priest for ever after the order of Melchisedec:) By so much was Jesus made a surety of a better testament. And they truly were many priests, because they were not suffered to continue by reason of death: But this *man*, because he continueth ever, hath an unchangeable priesthood. Wherefore he is able also to save them to the uttermost that come unto God by him, seeing he ever liveth to make intercession for them. For such an high priest became us, who is holy, harmless, undefiled, separate from sinners, and made higher than the heavens; Who needeth not daily, as those high priests, to offer up sacrifice, first for his own sins, and then for the people's: for this he did once, when he offered up himself. For the law maketh men high priests which have infirmity; but the word of the oath, which was since the law, maketh the Son, who is consecrated for evermore.

In Hebrews 8:1 (KJV) we read: Now of the things which we have spoken *this is* the sum: We have such an high priest, who is set on the right hand of the throne of the Majesty in the heavens;

He is the redeemer of all mankind and Savior of Israel. "I am the way, the truth and the life, no man cometh unto the Father but by me," says the Lord in John 14:6 (KJV).

The Fall of America and Judgment

I truly believe that next to Israel, America was the closest nation to the heart of God. Our laws and our constitution are based on the Bible. The first textbooks used in the schools of this country were from the Holy Bible. We did not become the greatest nation in the history of the world by accident.

Oh yes, there was a long period of slavery, but God raised up a man to change the course of things in that era, Abraham Lincoln. As for the inequalities that beset our nation sometime after, God raised up men such as Martin Luther King Jr. to prick the nation's conscious and tear down the walls of segregation and discrimination.

As long as our nation was moving toward being one of brotherhood, with liberty and justice for all, and we gave Him glory for being the one responsible for our status as leaders of the free world, we enjoyed His choicest blessings and prevailed against our enemies.

In Revelations 18:1-2 (KJV) John writes: And after these things I saw another angel come down from heaven, having great power; and the earth was lightened with his glory. And he cried mightily with a strong voice, saying, Babylon the great is fallen, is fallen, and is become the habitation of devils, and the hold of every foul spirit, and a cage of every unclean and hateful bird.

This friend is descriptive of present day America. In the last four or five decades we have seen morality hit rock bottom in our nation. One young woman was able to have prayer removed from the schools. As a child, I remember our school day beginning with the singing of the Lord's Prayer. During the course of study we sang songs such as America the Beautiful, I Come to the Garden, Come ye Thankful People, and other songs that glorified God.

We never dreamed of a day that shooting would be common place in the schools. When prayer went out then the devil came in with drugs, promiscuity and all manner of illicit lifestyles. Add to that the legal killing of the unborn, movies filled with sex and violence, and we have all the ingredients of a nation ready for God's judgment.

Proverbs 14:34 (KJV) reads: "Righteousness exalteth a nation: but sin *is* a reproach to any people."

Psalms 9:17 (KJV) reads: "The wicked shall be turned into hell, and all the nations that forget God."

A blind person can see that our nation has become a hell hole and people are afraid to even go out at night. Many are imprisoned in their own homes because of iron bars, chains, and locks which have caused many to perish in fires or other emergencies where escape time is crucial. Our major cities have become filled with gangs and thugs who have no respect at all for human life.

The Columbine school killings, Illinois shootings to name a few, there were others, some even in elementary schools should shake us up to seek the face of Almighty God to intervene. He is the only one that can change things.

Just in this month of April 2008, a mother turned her son in to authorities after finding a note with plans for him and others to plant explosives in the school. The fact that the students at Columbine were able to bring all of the weapons into the school without being detected is mind boggling.

How many times have we seen senseless acts of violence copied after movie depictions? When terrible things such as the Manson crimes happen, a movie is made which further glorifies this type of violence. It seems that America's movie goers are thirsting for violent blood and guts films. Even our young children are spending so much time playing war games. You hardly see a movie anymore that's not filled with machine gun fire, bomb explosions and of course sexually explicit scenes.

Can you just picture the Roman Coliseum filled to capacity with people cheering while men slew one another as gladiators, or as many Christians were torn to pieces by lions? They probably were eating snacks while they watched, just as people today enjoy popcorn and hot dogs at movies and sporting events.

The late Bishop W.T. Phillips warned us about this day. He spoke in the 1960's of the sex and violence on television. And that many children were watching and taking it in with a desire to act it out when they grew up. Well, it's coming to pass. Children are killing parents, parents are killing children and many say God told them to do it. Serial killers report that voices spoke to them. This is proof positive if you don't know the voice of God you are open to Satan's devices.

Everything that God made He saw as good and very good (Genesis 1). God made the earth for man to inhabit and enjoy the work of His hands. It was not the will of God for us to destroy one another and His creation. When sin came into the world then death and destruction followed.

Yet we find in John 3:16 (KJV): "For God so loved the world, that he gave his only begotten Son, that whosoever believeth in him should not perish, but have everlasting life."

My friends we have a remedy for all the things that beset our nation and our world. That remedy is Jesus Christ the Messiah of Israel and the Savior of the world. He is the deliverer and hope of glory to all that will trust Him. John 3:36 (KJV) says: "He that believeth on the Son hath everlasting life: and he that believeth not the Son shall not see life; but the wrath of God abideth on him."

Movie and television producers have been known to remark that a few Christians would not stop them from showing sexually explicit movies on television, and everywhere you turn the standards are being lowered. Homosexuals and lesbians have come out boldly in the open and some even profess to be followers of Christ. Some states are even trying to pass laws recognizing same sex marriages.

Hope of the Righteous

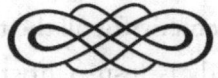

Oh, my friends, don't you see the times we are living in. But, there is hope for the people of God.

Daniel 12:10 (KJV) says; "Many shall be purified, and made white, and tried; but the wicked shall do wickedly: and none of the wicked shall understand; but the wise shall understand."

In Luke 17:26-30 (KJV), we find the words of our Lord and Savior Jesus Christ: And as it was in the days of Noe, so shall it be also in the days of the Son of man. They did eat, they drank, they married wives, they were given in marriage, until the day that Noe entered into the ark, and the flood came, and destroyed them all. Likewise also as it was in the days of Lot; they did eat, they drank, they bought, they sold, they planted, they builded; But the same day that Lot went out of Sodom it rained fire and brimstone from heaven, and destroyed *them* all. Even thus shall it be in the day when the Son of man is revealed.

Paul wrote to the church Romans 13:11-12 (KJV): And that, knowing the time, that now it is high time to awake out of sleep; for now is our salvation nearer than when we believed. The night is far spent, the day is at hand; Let us therefore cast off the works of darkness, and let us put on the armor of light.

It truly is time for the people of God to put on the whole armor of God that ye may be able to stand against the wiles of the devil (Ephesians 6:11).

Jesus warned in Matthews 24:11-14; And many false prophets shall rise, and shall deceive many. And because iniquity shall abound, the love of many shall wax cold. But He that shall endure unto the end, the same shall be saved. And this gospel of the Kingdom shall be preached in all the world for a witness unto all nations; and then shall the end come.

GREAT TRIBULATION

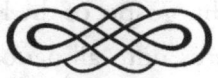

But prior to the end, He told of things that must come to past. Matthews 24:6-8 (KJV): And ye shall hear of wars and rumors of wars; see that ye be not troubled; for all these things must come to pass, but the end is not yet. For nation shall rise against Nation, and kingdom against kingdom; and there shall be famines, and pestilences, and earthquakes' in divers places. All these are the beginning of sorrows.

In Matthew 24:21-22 (KJV) we read: For then shall be great tribulation, such as was not since the beginning of the world to this time, no nor ever shall be. And except those days be shortened, there should no flesh be saved. But for the elects sake those days shall be shortened.

We will deal with that later on. Just be mindful that Jesus is saying without divine intervention man would destroy all life. That, my friends, is nuclear holocaust.

The mere suggestion that man would be capable of destroying all life on the planet could not be possible until the age of chemical and nuclear weapons. Poison gases were used in World War I but were outlawed afterwards. All the nations realized the deadly repercussions to all involved. World War II was fought without weapons of mass destruction until the development and use of the atomic bomb against Japan. The devastating results left a grim picture of what would happen if use of these weapons were put into play.

The cold war ensued as the two superpowers. The USA and the USSR faced off against each other. Let us remember that a new and much more powerful weapon (the hydrogen bomb) was in the arsenals. With each side having the means of destroying all life on the planet many times over, a sense of reasoning prevailed. So, a fragile peace has existed through treaties until now. The arms race continued as more modern ships, planes, and weaponry was devised.

TERRORISM

September 11, 2001 (commonly referred to as 9/11) was a wakeup call for America!

God let us see our vulnerability. With all our ships, planes, tanks, bombs and armies how susceptible we are to attack. No great power moved with force against us. The devil using a few men brought about this great tragedy.

A very noted religious leader when asked by government officials, "Why did God let this happen?" The response was, "I don't know." It grieved my heart and the hearts of many spirit-filled believers to hear those words. This was a warning from the Almighty and only a sample of what's to come if we don't turn to God as a nation with our whole heart.

Joel 2:12-13 (KJV) says: Therefore also now, saith the Lord, turn ye even to me with all your heart, and with fasting, and with weeping, and with mourning: And rend your heart, and not your garments, and turn unto the Lord your God: for He is gracious and merciful, slow to anger, and of great kindness, and repenteth him of the evil.

Let me get back to the vision. On a visit to Kiev, President Bush stated that one of His aims was to get the Ukraine (of which Kiev is the capital) and another nearby country Georgia into NATO (North Atlantic Treaty Organization). Now, we all know that NATO was formed after World War II as a shield against the Soviet Union, mainly Russia. After fighting as allies against Nazi Germany and fascist Italy, the USA, England, France and Germany recognized the ambitions of Soviet Russia to control Eastern Europe. Thus, NATO was set up and the cold war ensued.

The pace and the cost of the arms race was more than the USSR could stand and its economy collapsed. This resulted in many smaller Soviet bloc-nations opting for freedom and democracy. Even Russia showed signs of adopting the capitalist system but because of the state of the economy many desired the old way and Vladimir Putin became a prominent leader. With their vast oil and natural gas reserves they are once again a great power. That along with a renewed friendship with China has brought about a resurgence and willingness to flex their military might once again. Some described it as a marriage made in heaven. Russia has the technology and China the man power.

At this point, we want to note that along with the fall of the USSR and the tearing down of the Berlin Wall came the opportunity for many Jews to return back to their land. We find in Isaiah 11:12 (KJV), "And He shall set up an ensign for the nations, and shall assemble the outcast's of Israel, and gather together the dispersed of Judah from the four corners of the earth."

I knew a Jewish business man (now deceased) who showed me a flyer back in the 1980's concerning the raising of funds to get the Falasha Jews out of Ethiopia at a cost of $5,000 each. Shimon Peres who was once Israel's Prime Minister, said that they would not rest until all of their brothers and sisters were brought out of Ethiopia. Recently a noted television preacher was asking help of Christian believers to donate funds enabling Jews to be flown to Israel from Russia.

So, we see the signs of the end-time prophecies being fulfilled. After the soviet collapse it was aired that armaments of all types were being sold by Russia because of the need for cash. It was also reputed that some nuclear weapons were unaccounted for. One of the television networks did a story on the ex-Soviet satellite countries. We already know that terrorist groups would love to get their hands on such weaponry and would not hesitate to use them.

Let's go back to President Bush's visit to Kiev. He had made known that He wanted to put a missile defense system in these former USSR countries; hence, the need to get them into NATO. Not only did this proposal anger Vladimir Putin but it caused a stir in some western nations, notably, Germany and France which depend on Russia for oil and gas. Russia had turned off the spigot to some of its neighboring nations (I believe the Ukraine was one) over disagreement on pricing.

So, we see some Eastern and Western European countries are between a rock and a hard place. Couple that with the emergence of the European common market and the rise of the Euro and we can see American influence rapidly fading. Remember how close we came to nuclear war when Russia under Nikita Khrushchev tried to put missiles in Cuba. Will they permit us to do just that at their front door without going to war?

Our military now is stretched so thin what with Iraq and Afghanistan having our armed forces tied up for the most part, how could we deal with another major conflict? A few more major natural disasters such as hurricanes, earthquakes, tornadoes and the like could leave us vulnerable to a massive enemy strike. I don't believe they would attempt one while we are strong and alert, but if we're beset with massive problems we may not be able to repel a nuclear attack.

Our strategy has been; a strong defense will ward off an enemy attack. Let us not forget the rejoicing in the streets of Saudi Arabia (a friendly nation) after September 11, 2001 and one from which much of our oil is purchased. Many nations despise us because of our status in the earth. They envy us because we have been so abundantly blessed by God.

America's rise and prominence is attributed to one source and that is the Almighty. Many nations have their gods that they exalt, but our country has prospered and been blessed while so many others have faced famine, upheavals and despair.

Now, where Israel got in trouble with God was through learning the ways of the heathen nations which God strictly forbade. When they disobeyed they suffered the consequences. We allow immigrants to come here and demand that they be allowed freedom, not only to do as they please but to challenge our laws. In many of the countries from whence they came "Christianity" is forbidden and many believers have become martyrs.

We know the stated objective of Islam is to take over the world. We that have accepted the Gospel and have received the Spirit of Christ know how this is going to play out.

We find in Revelations 11:15 (KJV): "And the seventh angel sounded; and there were great voices in heaven, saying, the Kingdoms of this world are become the Kingdoms of our Lord and of His Christ; and He shall reign forever and ever."

In Revelations 20:6 (KJV): "Blessed and holy is He that hath part in the first resurrection; on such the second death hath no power, but they shall reign with Him a thousand years!"

This is the hope of the righteous. But, let us go back to the things which must first come to pass. We already have witnessed the restoration of Israel.

In Joel 3:1-2 (KJV) we read: for, behold, in those days, and in that time, when I shall bring again the captivity of Judah and Jerusalem. I will also gather all nations, and will bring them down into the valley of Jehoshaphat, and will plead with them there for my people and for my heritage Israel, whom they have scattered among the nations, and parted my land.

In Joel 3:12-15 (KJV) we read: Let the heathen be wakened, and come up to the valley of Jehoshaphat. For there will I sit to judge all the heathen

round about. Put ye in the sickle, for the harvest is ripe, come, get you down; for the press is full, the fats overflow; for their wickedness is great. Multitudes, multitudes in the valley of decision for the day of the Lord is near in the valley of decision. The sun and the moon shall be darkened, and the stars shall withdraw their shining. The Lord also shall roar out of Zion, and utter His voice from Jerusalem; and the heavens and the earth shall shake; but the Lord shall be the hope of His people; and the strength of the children of Israel.

In Psalms 2 (KJV) we read: "Why do the heathen rage and the people imagine a vain thing? The kings of the earth set themselves, and the rulers take counsel together against the Lord and against His anointed, saying, let us break their bands asunder and cast away their cords from us. He that sitteth in the heavens shall laugh: The Lord shall have them in derision. Then shall He speak unto them in His wrath, and vex them in His sore displeasure. Yet have I set my king upon my holy hill of Zion. I will declare the decree; the Lord hath said unto me, thou art my son; this day have I begotten thee. Ask of me, and I shall give thee the heathen for thine inheritance, and the uttermost parts of the earth for thy possession. Thou shall break them with a rod of iron; thou shall dash them in pieces like a potter's vessel."

Jesus in Revelation 2:26-27 (KJV): To the church of Thyatira said; And He that overcometh, and keepeth my works unto the end, to him will I give power over the nations. And he shall rule them with a rod of iron; as the vessels of a potter shall they be broken to shivers; even as I received of my father.

Friends, Jesus came as a meek and humble lamb the first time. He gave His life to ransom us from death and the grave. He also commanded us to be wise as serpents but harmless as doves.

Oh, but in His "second coming" it will be completely different. Jude wrote in verses 14 and 15 (KJV): And Enoch also the seventh from Adam, prophesied of these, saying, Behold the Lord cometh with ten thousands of His saints, to execute judgment upon all, and to convince all that are ungodly among them of all their ungodly deeds which they have ungodly committed, and of all their hard speeches which ungodly sinners have spoken against Him.

The Lord's second coming will be two fold. To put down His enemies, (all that do wickedness) and to set up His millennial kingdom on the earth. Only born again believers will rule and reign with Him. Of course, this is after the removal of the Antichrist and the binding of Satan for a thousand years.

The nineteenth chapter of Revelation gives us a graphic description of the war against the enemies of God and Israel and how their carcasses shall be eaten by the fowls of heaven. Some of the prophets spoke of how God will fight against and defeat His enemies. Let us look at some of their writings.

Let's begin with Zechariah 14:1-9 (KJV): Behold, the day of the LORD cometh, and thy spoil shall be divided in the midst of thee. For I will gather all nations against Jerusalem to battle; and the city shall be taken, and the houses rifled, and the women ravished; and half of the city shall go forth into captivity, and the residue of the people shall not be cut off from the city. Then shall the LORD go forth, and fight against those nations, as when he fought in the day of battle. And his feet shall stand in that day upon the mount of Olives, which *is* before Jerusalem on the east, and the mount of Olives shall cleave in the midst thereof toward the east and toward the west, *and there shall be* a very great valley; and half of the mountain shall remove toward the north, and half of it toward the south. And ye shall flee *to* the valley of the mountains; for the valley of the mountains shall reach unto Azal: yea, ye shall flee, like as ye fled from before the earthquake in the days of Uzziah king of Judah: and the LORD my God shall come, *and* all the saints with thee. And it shall come to pass in that day, *that* the light shall not be clear, *nor* dark: But it shall be one day which shall be known to the Lord, not day, nor night: but it shall come to pass, that at evening time it shall be light. 8 And it shall be in that day, that living waters shall go out from Jerusalem; half of them toward the former sea, and half of them toward the hinder sea: in summer and in winter shall it be. 9 And the Lord shall be king over all the earth: in that day shall there be one Lord, and his name one.

The Apostle Paul writing in Ephesians 4:5 (KJV) says, "One Lord, one faith, one baptism." Verse six says; "One God and Father of all, who is above all, and through all, and in you all."

This is talking about the believers, the redeemed. Let's go back to Zechariah 14:10-12 (KJV): All the land shall be turned as a plain from Geba to Rimmon south of Jerusalem; and it shall be lifted up and inhabited in her place, from Benjamins gate unto the place of the first gate, unto the corner gate, and from the tower of Hananeel unto the king's wine presses. And men shall dwell in it, and there shall be no more utter destruction; but Jerusalem shall be safely inhabited. And this shall be the plague where with the Lord will smite all the people that have fought against Jerusalem; their flesh shall consume a way while they stand upon their feet, and their eyes shall consume away in their holes, and their tongue shall consume away in their mouth.

This I believe is the result of nuclear radiation. Let us go back to Ezekiel 38:18-22 (KJV): And it shall come to pass at the same time when Gog shall come against the land of Israel, saith the Lord GOD, *that* my fury shall come up in my face. For in my jealousy *and* in the fire of my wrath have I spoken, Surely in that day there shall be a great shaking in the land of Israel; So that the fishes of the sea, and the fowls of the heaven, and the beasts of the field, and all creeping things that creep upon the earth, and all the men that *are* upon the face of the earth, shall shake at my presence, and the mountains shall be thrown down, and the steep places shall fall, and every wall shall fall to the ground. And I will call for a sword against him throughout all my mountains, saith the Lord GOD: every man's sword shall be against his brother. And I will plead against him with pestilence and with blood; and I will rain upon him, and upon his bands, and upon the many people that *are* with him, an overflowing rain, and great hailstones, fire, and brimstone.

Let's look at Ezekiel 39:4 (KJV); "Thou shalt fall upon the mountains of Israel, thou, and all thy bands, and the people that is with thee: I will give thee unto the ravenous birds of every sort, and to the beast of the field to be devoured."

BLACK GOLD

Let's take a look at probably the biggest issue in the world today. That, my friend is "oil." It is said that, "Whoever controls the oil, controls the world."

About 1972, I remember listening to a radio talk show in Chicago and hearing someone say that the main reason for the USA being in Vietnam was that there was oil off the coast. After the pull out and the withdrawal of American troops this fact was revealed, although some years later. I believe that most Americans are convinced the reason our armed forces are in Iraq is oil. The ruse of fighting for freedom and to establish democracy doesn't hold water.

When we look at history we know that resources whatever they were; gold, rubber, other minerals, ivory, rare spices and things of value, and of course oil, was the real reasoning for subjecting third and fourth world countries to servitude going back probably hundreds if not thousands of years.

So we see that oil at this point in history is not only important but is very necessary to fuel the industries, armed forces and the civilian needs of the

Now, fast forward to Revelation 19:11-21 (KJV): And I saw heaven opened, and behold a white horse; and he that sat upon him *was* called Faithful and True, and in righteousness he doth judge and make war. His eyes *were* as a flame of fire, and on his head *were* many crowns; and he had a name written, that no man knew, but he himself. And he *was* clothed with a vesture dipped in blood: and his name is called The Word of God. And the armies *which were* in heaven followed him upon white horses, clothed in fine linen, white and clean. And out of his mouth goeth a sharp sword, that with it he should smite the nations: and he shall rule them with a rod of iron: and he treadeth the winepress of the fierceness and wrath of Almighty God. And he hath on *his* vesture and on his thigh a name written, KING OF KINGS, AND LORD OF LORDS. And I saw an angel standing in the sun; and he cried with a loud voice, saying to all the fowls that fly in the midst of heaven, Come and gather yourselves together unto the supper of the great God; That ye may eat the flesh of kings, and the flesh of captains, and the flesh of mighty men, and the flesh of horses, and of them that sit on them, and the flesh of all *men, both* free and bond, both small and great. And I saw the beast, and the kings of the earth, and their armies, gathered together to make war against him that sat on the horse, and against his army. And the beast was taken, and with him the false prophet that wrought miracles before him, with which he deceived them that had received the mark of the beast, and them that worshipped his image. These both were cast alive into a lake of fire burning with brimstone. And the remnant were slain with the sword of him that sat upon the horse, which *sword* proceeded out of his mouth: and all the fowls were filled with their flesh.

This ushers in the millennial rule of Jesus on the earth. In Revelation 20:1-15 (KJV) we read: And I saw an angel come down from heaven, having the key of the bottomless pit and a great chain in his hand. And he laid hold on the dragon, that old serpent, which is the

Devil, and Satan, and bound him a thousand years, And cast him into the bottomless pit, and shut him up, and set a seal upon him, that he should deceive the nations no more, till the thousand years should be fulfilled: and after that he must be loosed a little season. And I saw thrones, and they sat upon them, and judgment was given unto them: and *I saw* the souls of them that were beheaded for the witness of Jesus, and for the word of God, and which had not worshipped the beast, neither his image, neither had received *his* mark upon their foreheads, or in their hands; and they lived and reigned with Christ a thousand years. But the rest of the dead lived not again until the thousand years were finished. This *is* the first resurrection. Blessed and holy *is* he that hath part in the first resurrection: on such the second death hath no power, but they shall be priests of God and of Christ, and shall reign with him a thousand years. And when the thousand years are expired, Satan shall be loosed out of his prison, And shall go out to deceive the nations which are in the four quarters of the earth, Gog and Magog, to gather them together to battle: the number of whom *is* as the sand of the sea. And they went up on the breadth of the earth, and compassed the camp of the saints about, and the beloved city: and fire came down from God out of heaven, and devoured them. And the devil that deceived them was cast into the lake of fire and brimstone, where the beast and the false prophet *are*, and shall be tormented day and night for ever and ever. And I saw a great white throne, and him that sat on it, from whose face the earth and the heaven fled away; and there was found no place for them. **12**And I saw the dead, small and great, stand before God; and the books were opened: and another book was opened, which is *the book* of life: and the dead were judged out of those things which were written in the books, according to their works. And the sea gave up the dead which were in it; and death and hell delivered up the dead which were in them: and they were judged every man according to their works. And death and hell were cast into the lake of fire. This is the second death. And whosoever was not found written in the book of life was cast into the lake of fire.

Now, we come to the inheritance of the righteous. John declared in Revelation 21:1-8 (KJV); And I saw a new heaven and a new earth: for the first heaven and the first earth were passed away; and there was no more sea. And I John saw the holy city, new Jerusalem, coming down from God out of heaven, prepared as a bride adorned for her husband. And I heard a great voice out of heaven saying, Behold, the tabernacle of God *is* with men, and he will dwell with them, and they shall be his people, and God himself shall be with them, *and be* their God. And God shall wipe away all tears from their eyes; and there shall be no more death, neither sorrow, nor crying, neither shall there be any more pain: for the former things are passed away. And he that sat upon the throne said, Behold, I make all things new. And he said unto me, Write: for these words are true and faithful. And he said unto me, it is done. I am Alpha and Omega, the beginning and the end. I will give unto him that is athirst of the fountain of the water of life freely. He that overcometh shall inherit all things; and I will be his God, and he shall be my son. But the fearful, and unbelieving, and the abominable, and murderers, and whoremongers, and sorcerers, and idolaters, and all liars, shall have their part in the lake which burneth with fire and brimstone: which is the second death.

My friends, this is the final consummation of the wicked and the inheritance of the "over-comers". Remember Jesus said in John 16:33 (KJV), "These things I have spoken unto you, that in me ye might have peace. In the world ye shall have tribulation; but be of good cheer: I have overcome the world." In the world ye shall have tribulation. He came to be our example and to let us know that we can overcome the world not walking in the flesh but in the spirit. That's why in John 3:3 He said. "ye must be born again." John 3:5 tells us, "except a man be born of water, and of the spirit, he cannot enter into the Kingdom of God." That's why it is so important to be washed in the blood and filled with the Holy Ghost (Acts 2:38).

Paul tells us in Romans 8:9-14 (KJV): But ye are not in the flesh, but in the Spirit, if so be that the Spirit of God dwell in you. Now if any man have not the Spirit of Christ, he is none of his. And if Christ *be* in you, the body *is* dead because of sin; but the Spirit *is* life because of righteousness. But if the Spirit of him that raised up Jesus from the dead dwell in you, he that raised up Christ from the dead shall also quicken your mortal bodies by his Spirit that dwelleth in you. Therefore, brethren, we are debtors, not to the flesh, to live after the flesh. For if ye live after the flesh, ye shall die: but if ye through the Spirit do mortify the deeds of the body, ye shall live. For as many as are led by the Spirit of God, they are the sons of God.

This, my friends, is the only plan in the Holy Scriptures whereby we may obtain eternal life.

CHINA EMERGES AS A GREAT NATION

China is rapidly becoming a major force in Angola, Brazil, and other African nations as well as Cambodia. With a surplus of money earned through the selling of huge amounts of goods made by a large labor force cheaply.

In August 2008, South Ossetia began fighting in Georgia as capital of separatists and was attacked by Georgian forces. Russia says this proves Georgia can not be trusted and NATO should reconsider admitting them into NATO. The rebel forces are backed by Russia who seems to be on a course to restoring the USSR, at least in part. Ossetia is a break away province of Georgia with leaning toward Russia. This fighting occurring after a truce agreement; each side blames the other for starting the fight.

On August 8, 2008, Georgia claimed to have shot down four Russian jets. Bear in mind, Georgia is a declared ally of the United States though it is a former satellite of the Soviet-bloc. The United States said it was sending negotiators to press for an immediate cease fire. This is a very flammable situation that could spread and drag the USA and Russia into a conflagration. This is at a time when we are bogged down in Iraq and Afghanistan. Our military has already admitted that it is stretched too thin. Does this mean if another major conflict arose we would be forced to use Nuclear Weapons?

It is reported that Russian tanks were moving into the breakaway province. The government of Georgia is appealing to the USA for help, stating that Russia is waging war against them.

Russian forces strike deep into Georgia and are not showing any sign of a rapid pullout. American ships are moving into the black sea and American planes are flying in humanitarian supplies. Seems like the Old Berlin scenario all over again. After closing roads leading to Berlin, Russia didn't dare fire upon the USA planes that participated in the Airlift. They knew we had the A-bomb and would use it. Poland agrees to let NATO missiles be stationed there for defensive purposes. Poland seems eager to do so as a guard against aggressive or rogue nations, meaning Russia or Iran.

As a result of Poland agreeing to the stationing of American defensive missiles on their territory, Russia has declared they are making themselves a target. Would they be willing to make a preemptive strike on Poland as Israel and maybe the USA is considering making on Iran.

During the Cuban Missile crisis President John F. Kennedy commanded the Navy to sink any Russian vessel that tried to run the blockade. He also stated that if a missile was fired from Cuba against any western hemisphere nation, the USA would consider it as an attack on itself and will respond with a full retaliation on the USSR.

Now that the tables are turned and the missiles are being placed in their front yard, will they become or have they already become fearful that with all these anti-soviet countries on their borders, it could incite revolution in Russia itself?

So now, they are speaking out more menacingly and boasting that they are not afraid and are willing to meet any confrontation from the west. This sounds like the bear is getting riled! On August 26, 2008, an English diplomat went to Kiev to assure Ukrainians that Britain would stand with them.

Are the Russians ready to risk all out war with the west? Or do they believe that pressure from the European nations that depend on them for oil and gas will be the mediating force? At any rate, it seems

that "Stalinism" is on the rise again. The question is who will back down.

On August 27, 2008, Russia announced they have developed a long range missile that can fly under the radar of the missile defense system to be set up in Poland. This is obviously a smack at the USA who is the maker of the missile defense system. Sounds like a bullying tactic?

Are they saying that the USA and the Western Europe allies have enough nuclear weapons in submarines, naval, and Air Force bases to reduce Russia to rubble? Any exchange would be devastating to either side. But, if God has allowed them to receive this kind of a mind set and to carry it out, how long before eruption takes place and the LORD himself has to step in to save mankind from self destruction?

We might add that Vladimir Putin is accusing the USA of provoking the Georgia Russian conflict. With the upcoming 2008 Presidential Election, we will see how things play out.

**Dr. William Standifer Sr
Pastor & Prophet
(1938-2021)**

ABOUT THE AUTHOR

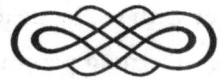

The late Pastor William Standifer has always been a vision driven vessel of God. His salvation was the result of his search for a better way of life. One night while praying, he asked God to show him this better way if there be any. He saw a vision on his bedroom ceiling of the hand of an angel that wrote the words REPENT in all caps. Immediately the Holy Bible opened up and was sparkling gold. God revealed to him that if he wanted a better life, he had to obey God's Word.

A short time after this vision he was witnessed to by a coworker on his job, and was invited to attend a service. Pastor Standifer received Christ Jesus as his Lord and Savior on March 31, 1964 and later received the gift of the Holy Ghost. Shortly after he joined the church, he led his wife and 5 step children to join. They all received salvation through Jesus Christ. Pastor Standifer was appointed and later licensed as Deacon and served many years. After having 2 biological children, William Standifer Jr and Juanita Standifer, he accepted his call into ministry1983. He worked tirelessly assisting and building the ministries of various churches for several years and afterwards became the pastor of his own mission called "The Living Word" in both Calumet City and Harvey, Illinois.

In 2002, he was ordained Elder and assigned to be Pastor of Evergreen A.O. H. Church of God in Memphis, TN. He pastored faithfully there until May 2020. After becoming ill, he relocated to Atlanta Georgia and lived with his daughter, Dr. Juanita (Standifer) Woodson and son in law Warren Woodson. He passed away peacefully surrounded by his loving family on December 24th, 2021.

Although he is no longer with us, his teachings and prophecies live on! He "wrote the vision" concerning prophecies he received from the Lord that helped explain the events surrounding the coming of Jesus Christ, and the importance of salvation, so many would know the truth and run with it!